OUR LADY OF EUROPE

For Frank
with best wishes
Jeremy Hooker
11. 6. 97

Other Enitharmon Books by Jeremy Hooker

Soliloquies of a Chalk Giant (1974)

David Jones: An Exploratory Study of the Writings (1975)

Landscape of the Daylight Moon (1978)

John Cowper Powys and David Jones:
A Comparative Study (1979)

(Editor) Frances Bellerby, Selected Stories (1986)

Master of the Leaping Figures (1987)

Their Silence a Language (1993)

JEREMY HOOKER

Our Lady of Europe

London
ENITHARMON PRESS
1997

First published in 1997
by the Enitharmon Press
36 St George's Avenue
London N7 0HD

Distributed in Europe
by Password (Books) Ltd
23 New Mount Street
Manchester, M4 4DE

Distributed in the USA and Canada
by Dufour Editions Inc.
PO Box 7, Chester Springs
PA 19425, USA

ISBN 1 900564 15 7

British Library Cataloguing-in-Publication Data.
A catalogue record for this book is available
from the British Library.

Typeset in 10pt Bembo by Bryan Williamson, Frome
and printed in Great Britain by
The Cromwell Press, Broughton Gifford, Wiltshire

Acknowledgements

Some of these poems first appeared in *Agenda, An Enitharmon Anthology, Between the Severn and the Wye, The Haiku Quarterly, Modern Painters, New Welsh Review, Planet, PN Review, The Poetry Book Society Anthology 1987-1988, Poetry Wales, Proceedings of the First North American Conference on Welsh Studies, Red Brick Review, The Poet's Voice, The Swansea Review.* An earlier version of 'Edvard Munch: *The Sick Child'* appeared in *With a Poet's Eye*: A Tate Gallery Anthology. *In Praise of Windmills* was published in a limited edition, with images by Tony Nesbit, by Circle Press. The first and last parts of 'That trees are men walking' were incorporated in my programme *A Map of David Jones*, first broadcast on BBC Radio 3 on 5 November 1995.

Contents

1 *A Troy of the North*

2 *Written in clay*

A TROY OF THE NORTH

To Mieke

All day the stillness
of a storm that will not break.
After sudden violence of downpour,
thunderclap, the same clouds
shutting out the hills,
the sea a grey flagstone
at the town's back door.

The shadow of my hand
moved on the paper
heavily, marking
the space between us.
I sensed you far off,
in a deeper stillness.

If I were Dafydd
I would send my seagull
over the Welsh mountains,
across England and the North Sea.
Where you lie with eyes open
in the dark it would come to you,
bringing love and sleep.

Beginning again

Walking in the New Year,
blinded with splinters
of rain, almost blown
off the dyke into the sea,

there is no one behind us
in all the wide land
but a frantic scarecrow
dressed in a black suit
and running, running, running.

Lines for an ice-book

In one night
the privet hedge
is turned to glass.
The birches shatter
or bend into hoops.

So the cold makes images:
it finds for living things
the exact,
the deathly equivalent.

Ice bark coats the springing tree;
translucent, ice wombs
cradle buds.

I see for the first time
what the old Welsh poet meant:
a man could stand on a blade of grass.

Willem Barents' last voyage

(after Gerrit de Veer)

Past Fair Isle, we saw
a wondrous sign:
the sun, with a sun
on either hand, all
circled by a rainbow.

But after, sailing
the way of the north
we found Spitsbergen,
and crosses on a sea
of ice and darkness.

★

A bear, a white bear
on an island.
Blood in the sea,
and a bear swimming away
with an axe stuck in it.
We hacked its head to pieces,
we skinned it, and ate it,
but it didn't taste good.
We called our new land
        Bear Island.

★

Not a smell of Cathay,
but a sea spouting
whales & walruses –
possibilities
of commodity & utility
for those who further
and set forward ventures.

If we return
we will be a wonder –
men in caps of white fox fur
in rich Amsterdam.

*

Sun's absence, moon's light.
Our sand-clock's stuck to the floor
of our driftwood haven.
Bears claw at the roof,
skin sticks to iron.

We lie under snow and hear
ice crack,
out of the track of time.

*

He was our chief guide and only pilot
on whom we reposed our selves,
next under God.
'Gerrit,' he said, 'lift me up.
I must see the ice-cap again.'
He was looking at the map when
his eyes turned in his head and he died.

Nostalgia

This morning,
as I opened the blinds
of the living room,
the sight of gulls
wheeling and diving
over a patch of civic grass
took me in an instant
out of the brick city
and across country
to the dyke,
the grey waters of the North Sea.
And again, over the sea
in one flight, on
to the mud-flats and salt-grass,
all that litters the shore of childhood.

A Troy of the North

for Alan Clodd

Seagulls mewing over reedy ditches,
but no one to sing the deeds, nothing

to tell the tale of a people
who did the work left undone
on the third day of Creation –

who shaped a mound of clay
on salt-marsh, and made
pasture at the brink of the sea.

Storm tides covered it,
over and over, spreading silt,
clogging ditches with corpses.
And what the sea did not drown
the Northmen burnt,
leaving blood-flecked foam
and homesteads blazing on the flood.

And again, over
and over again,
they took the measure
of water, and the weight
of clay, and raised the mound.

Nothing to tell
but a seawall far inland,
a dyke in the middle of fields,
cattle wading in summer pasture
and plots where hay lies
in windrows, like coarse yellow hair.

Bones dug into the earth,
site over site,
black earth and ashes
and the clay of makers and beasts.

And on the island raised above fields
that still smell of the sea,
the church of John the Baptist,
old red brick like dried blood
on a green hill, the tower
beside the body, a severed head.

Cloudscape

for Adam Hopkins

Wind-sculpted, white clouds
tower over us.

They are icebergs following
the route of the glaciers.

What are we doing standing
and looking up – tiny
on a flat ocean of clay –
if not to appreciate
what hills and mountains are?

A new love poem

for Mieke

A new earth
where not long ago was sea.

How do the moles know?
Already they snout in pale grey
sandy soil full of shells.

There is a poetry of dykes
against the sky –
a church spire – a windmill.
It is beautiful, and bodes peace.

Clods of earth cling to the flesh
of beets waiting in long mounds.
The unpicked cabbages
have a strangely expectant look.

Someone has lit a fire
in a corner of the day.

Red flames leap;
yellow reeds pierce the air.
But over all grey drifts down,
like silt clouding still water.

This is a poetry I know,
since you give it me.

In praise of windmills

In the north the windmills stand
roundly on land and by water.

I take a leaf from the Windmill Psalter.
I name them, both the little and the great:

Young Hendrick and Four Winds,
Goliath and The Helper.

They have come far, but seem
to have grown where they are,
as native to the Netherlands
as sarsens to Salisbury Plain,
and as worthy of praise.

Yet Quixote was right;
they are monstrous.

                    If windmills
did not exist, Hieronymus
Bosch would have dreamt them.
They are living contraptions,
part insect and part bird;
mechanical creatures pondering
flight; earthbound,
flailing at heaven.

There are windmills in the mind,
alive to every breath of fear.

And things that hold firm:
cross-beams and quarter-bars,
crown-tree and king-post;
windmills that drive
and are driven, turning
indifferent winds to use.

They are labourers
at the brink of water;
old warhorses
that take the starving field.

No wonder people say,
The miller is a mighty man;
his hand spans earth and sky.
The great sails are dancing
but the painter holds them still.

The polder is a blank page
marked with a cross:
                    Goliath,
a little windmill but a giant
graced by need and by use,
solitary as a lighthouse
on a sea of blue clay,
in a land raised from the sea.

Over furrow and rhine,
I see the blade of a sail
shining, and think of voyages,
and stillness at the heart
of tumbling breakers
where the keel strikes home.

Behind the dyke the wind blasts
and the sea hungers.

Here the windmill stands
roundly by water and on land.

I take a leaf from the Windmill Psalter.
May the grace of the sails breathe in my song.

Noordpolderzijl

1

On one side of the dyke
a long, narrow road points
towards the far horizon.
Herons fish in ditches beside the road.
Ploughed fields flow away inland.

On the other side,
a long, narrow channel
pointing out to sea,
fishing boats moored
between green pastures.
Cows share the last grass with gulls.

2

A sluice, a handful
of red-brick houses –
but the place feels like the end
of a continent, somewhere
to sail from, over the rim.

What is it like to stay:
to live with the distances,
to lie down and wake at the level
of tides, listening, feeling
the pressures of the sea?

For generations, one family
has kept the sluice.

What keeps them, perhaps,
is *polderlust*:
a deep, slow rhythm
that ebbs and flows,
changing the sea to land,
and the land to sea,

and sometimes a quickness –
skim of the first swallow,
oystercatchers abandoning
the mud for the sky, piping,
dancing their mating dance
over the edge of the world.

Still-life

After long labour the place
is a patchwork of water and earth –
a broken mirror that shows the sky.

Slowly the brick walls crack,
the thatched, camel-backed houses
fall and are built again
on the same site, to the same design.

You see nothing of this,
drowsing on a wooden bridge
on an afternoon in late summer –
only rowan berries reddening
among leafy branches in peat-brown water.

The soil exudes a faint
hot-house smell and everything
is still, so still

that if a conker should fall
it would land with a thud
that rends walls, fissures the ground
and shakes the place to its foundations.

Ikons, autumn colours

Brown, yellow, gold – leaves
fall on the canal, on decks
of barges and houseboats,
on the brick streets.
In the exhibition
the colours deepen, darken.
Autumn, it seems, is part
of the eternal comedy
and the streets are everlasting.
The baby Jesus is held up
in a blanket by a team
of apostles and saints.
We look into the eye of Hell.
There is one pattern, whole
in every detail, that loses
no one, and no one escapes.
Brown, yellow, gold – leaves
fall on water, on decks
and the brick streets.
Deeper, darker, the ikons
smoulder and burn.

In the market

I wake from a dream of death as falling endlessly through darkness.

Later, in the market, we stream along slowly with the crowd.

A girl chats to a customer while her fingers expertly fill and tie a bag.

Her skill gives me pleasure.

Men in white overalls shave slices off round, yellow cheeses and hand them to us to taste.

How shapely the fruit and vegetables, how firmly they fill out their skins.

Gradually I reinhabit my body.

Among all the fish with sightless eyes, the eels, in yellow plastic crates, are still alive.

They move their bodies against each other slowly, coiling and uncoiling.

I imagine a terrible gasping.

Something deep inside me, dull-flickering, dreams of breathing in the depths of the sea.

Riposte to Michelangelo

'. . . landscapes, and little figures
here and there.'

They have bricks to build with,
green pasture and the shade of trees.
Their bridges span still waters.

In the market, a man slices a fish
without pausing in his talk.
People handle fruit and cheeses.
Scales confirm measurements
made by hand and eye.

In the country,
thick, green water
mirrors creamy elder blossom
and bright blue flowers.
The sun winks on black pantiles.

God so made the world
according to the old masters –
                broken men
who painted the substance
of things made whole,
as it was in the first place.

In their landscape,
light is material;
it does not divide,
it does not dissolve,
but renders soul to body,
                  body to soul.

Who is so little that he lacks
a place at the feast?

Starting early

We are disembodied spirits
of before-dawn dark. Our white faces
belong with the moons of platform clocks.

Outside, through the image
of our compartment travelling
beside us, we see an older country –

ages of candlelight glowing
under humped roofs set far apart,
where farmers rise in rooms
warmed by the breath of beasts.

Our baseless, fragile image
fades. Trees emerge against
deepening, smoke-blue distance –

remnants of the great forests
that still stand on earth.

Westerbork

To the memory of Etty Hillesum

1

Our path lies along the Milky Way
and from planet to planet –

then out from the trees
and past the grey saucers
of the radio telescope.

Among toadstools, under oaks
loaded with acorns, we find
a solitary, white earth-star.

2

A few late foxgloves on a bank –
'sheltered'
I say, and the word echoes oddly.

Who can resist the ironies?
When will we recognise
that irony is not enough?

3

How understand the faces, Etty?
You looked at them
from behind a window
and were terrified.

You sank to your knees speaking
the words that reign over life
and bind you to these men
in the depths:

'And God made man after His likeness.'

Did you know they would murder you
and your kind?
That they would drive even the children
into hiding, and hunt them down.
And the patients. And the doctors.
All would be sent out on the Tuesday morning train.

4

The black train, which an artist
in the camp painted, looming.

But what amazes more
is his painting of a typical farm
and farmyard beyond the wire
as he saw them,
as we see them still.

5

At first there is little to show –
a few irregularities in the ground
of what might be a park.

Then we see what we expect:
a wooden guard-post,
preserved, or perhaps restored.

Below it, a short stretch
of the railway track reaches
from buffers towards the east;
broken off, twisted, the rusted iron
curves into the air.

And there, incised in stone,
a verse from Lamentations.

6

They hunt our steps, that
we cannot go in our squares . . .

You were a fountain of life.
Your love flowed into the world.

You looked for meaning
and found it even in the worst,
accepting 'all as one mighty whole'.

But the faces – how shall we accept
that you could see in them
instruments of destiny?

Whose faces, Etty?
What are they like?

7

Back from the universe,
back from the world,
back from the streets
of Amsterdam,
back from the houses,
back from the rooms
and the rooms behind the rooms,

you were driven, and driven in.

The space of your freedom
was at last a book, in which you wrote,
passionate to understand;

a mind behind the white face;
a card, thrown from the train window:
'we have left the camp singing.'

Reigersbos

Up in the wind, we hear a noise
of stick knocking on stick, a retching,
and looking up see long beaks,
long black hairs like antennae,
hunched figures, cloaked in grey feathers.

No longer the familiars
of ditch or dyke,
or bird flying east, flying west.
No more the hunter stick-still
at the lip of a rhine,
or the ancient one – pterodactyl
rising suddenly in evening light,
or statuesque on a rusting barge
moored under city walls.

Not now fishers
of common margins,
but strangers, rocking
on rafts of branches and twigs.

High in the wind, on tree crowns
echoing rounded, bright-edged cloud,
they clack their beaks
and look down at us with yellow eyes.

And what are we who gaze back,
wanderers over the brink of our own world
who have stumbled into theirs.

In Drenthe

for Rutger Kopland

1

A May morning
when oak buds prick into leaf
and the peewits tumble and cry.
Downriver, faintly, the cuckoo.

It is not what we expect
when a greenshank flying down
from a fence post lifts its wings
to reveal white feathers, and is,
for that moment, an angel.

And surely the only one in this country
where the river flows rippling,
pulsing, and the sun kindles
the powdery sand, and beats
with white fire in the water.

It is more than we expect
and more and again more, when
the woods open on a meadow
yellow with dandelions
and you say, simply, 'It is a gift'.

2

Autumn, and the greeny, dark
river carries grass and leaves,
flowing slowly,
serpentine through meadows.

The glaciers crawled so far
and left the granite boulders
and the sandy ridge, the Dogsback.

And here the megaliths came
with the Neolithic track –
empty tombs, dark-gleaming.

In the blue sky, a daylight moon.
In the woods, toadstools –
red-capped, yellow, grey.
Stinkhorn, erect with shining skin
or half-eaten by flies.

So much to see, so much
to taste and touch.
But also a spirit that eludes –
in the light just so
on red leaf and yellow leaf
spinning, turning slowly,
as though each chooses to fall.

Island cemetery

Within sound of the surf,
lapped in the sand of Grey Monk Island,
lie the dead of two wars and many nations.

From white headstones,
each at an angle, looking up,
the named and the nameless speak:

A. Wilson/Wireless op./Air Gunner/Age 18.
Master J.O. Roberts/S.S. *Firth Fisher.*
Sergeant Borret and Walter Weizel.
Ein Deutscher Soldat.
Inconnu. Mort Pour La France.
A Soldier of the Great War.
Known Unto God.

How tidily their graves are kept,
sheltered in a hollow among dunes,
each plot filled with cockle shells,
sea-washed, white and blue,
under the sign of the cross.

How orderly the lines,
how clean the words that speak to us
of the dead.
It is right to honour them.

We are stilled, hearing only
a faint bee-hum and the wash of the sea.
A salt air mingles with resin from Scots Pines
and a scent of roses.

Then we hear the birds –
oystercatchers, curlews, gulls –
all the different voices.
Shelduck fly over, long necks outstretched.
A harrier scours marsh beyond the dunes.

This is their world, and was
in the beginning – the same and again the same,
where they pipe and shrill and cry
whether monks keep the hours
or bunkers are built on the sand
and the dead wash ashore or drop from the sky,
mangled and burnt.

The sand does not quake; blood
does not cry out from the ground.
Only now we are not at ease
with a peace we have not won,
imagining an earth cleansed
of hatred of nations,
with a beauty that deceives the living
and simplifies the dead.

Blinded

When I stumbled upon it, I was thinking about seeing: how the eye can devour, feeding secretly on all it sees, or chooses to see.

It was in a clearing among the trees. A sculpture carved from a block of white stone. It represented a figure which was both beast and man, seated at a table, or rather attached to it, for table and figure were carved from the same block. The table was like any administrator's, and the creature's shaggy paw-like hands and forearms rested on it, as he sat hunched, staring.

The head was rounded, and more pathetic than brutal.

What held me, though, was the face.

Someone had smeared the empty eye-sockets with a dark substance, which ran crookedly down across the cheeks, as if the creature had been savagely blinded.

After Rembrandt: *Saul and David*

The beautiful young man plays,
absorbed in the music he is making.

And the king listens –
there is only a curtain between them,
he could reach out,
touch David on the shoulder,
speak his love.

Saul hears, and his face
is haggard, stricken.
The music is close –
he could reach out,
he could touch the strings –
but he hears it where he sits,
deep inside himself,
music he was once part of,
that sounds now
eternally distant,
beyond the ramparts of paradise.

After Rembrandt: *The Anatomical Lesson*

It is one life
that shines in the dark eyes
of the surgeons who are bending
over the cadaver –
one life, unique in each.

The eyes of the dead man
are closed, his mouth
slightly open –
the mystery
has left this dead flesh

but shows in the eyes of the living,
in those who look down
at the exposed tendon,
the dissected arm,
or thoughtfully aside,

and in the face of the man
who looks at us,
wondering about himself,
mystified.

It is not yet only
a scientific question
that dawns in his dark eyes.

What is man? What am I
who am wonderfully
and fearfully made,
like this dead thing?

Vincent

In the north
he goes among the people,
farmers, women who cut the peat.
He is a peasant-painter labouring
to paint peasants.

He is somewhere in the room
with them, struggling to paint
the hands they dig with,
and put in the dish, and share out their portion.

Darkness
comes out of the earth in the north.
It moulds the figures,
it shapes the farms.
This is the good soil of Holland,
the soil the poor live on.
It means hardship, not misery,
not the dry, dusty wind of the Borinage.
The cold wall of the church
chills him to the spine,
he is a servant
of the man-forsaken god,
a light-bringer
who loves the dark.

Earth is new in the south – bright yellow,
vermilion, burgundy, violet,
sky blue, bright green.
Earth melts, burns with a flame
that does not destroy but restores.
This is the force life lives by,
the force he seeks to enter.

The sun roars in the harvest field.
He holds the yellow note,
the black cypress is a vortex
and the heavens rain down fire.

Gauguin paints him painting sunflowers,
in which he sees himself 'gone mad'.

He paints irises in the asylum garden,
tongues wagging, the silence
loud with shouts and screams.

He has gone out of hearing,
he is somewhere deep in the fields,

a stranger in a foreign land.

Rotterdam: Zadkine's *De Verwoeste Stad*

1

Bronze Atlas, with a mortal wound.

But still powerful:
a contorted giant, hands raised,
reeling in agony. Not defeated.

He is the city that will live again
when a bird builds its nest in the place
of his burnt-out heart.

2

When he was a boy
our friend saw the sculpture
lying in pieces, waiting
to be assembled and raised.

Now he often leaves his office
during the day, and walks on the waterfront
watching the ships.

He thinks of his father and grandfather,
of the river that will go on
when he is dead,
and he feels glad to be
'a minor part of it, but a part'.

Does he know how much rests upon him?

How lightly he shoulders this world.

Dreaming of Europe: a collage

How good our nights and days
of making love on the roof garden
among spires and towers
lilfted up on a level with clock faces
we did not see

★

THIS COULD BE A PLACE OF HISTORICAL IMPORTANCE

He has a taste for ambiguity
which he inscribes in stone paving
in front of the cathedral:

1. Something happened here you should know about.
Do not spit or dance on the spot.
Cover your head.

2. It is just possible that something important might happen here.

3. Think about it.
You could change the world.

★

It is certain that when she was a little girl
the big, black thing frightened her.

Now we are overawed,
the blackened stone spires
look down on us.

Inside, the upsurge of power,
graceful, light.

It is invested with a presence:
the after-image of bomb damage.

How many did it save?

★

It is impossible to leave the parapets of Europe.
You cannot abandon the fathers,
they come after you with retorts and muskets,
scissors and rolls of cloth.

You may trek across deserts
or sail over the rim of the world,
but the germ is in you.

                    Even in dreams
columns of water thunder to the ground,
cities are swept away.

Or a white wolf sits in a walnut tree
outside the window, looking in.

★

I believe in the head of Hans Arp.

It is a potato or an apple
or some good fruit he grew
from the tree of his imagination.

★

We learn to walk with the Christ child
on a walking-frame.

With a windmill, he teaches us to play.

He opens his arms with the generosity
of a drunkard.

Magnified in the minds of men
he becomes a demon who drinks our blood.

★

I believe in Hans Arp and Sophie Taeuber
and the visitation of angels.

Angels are no economists.
Magnificently
they squander the light.

★

Does the wood see, does the field?

It is not after all the worst thought
that no one watches, spying
into every shell-hole and crack.

★

Longing is the road they travel.

Every one a stranger
searching for the lost home.

It is not here, not there.

★

After they were driven out
they sought shelter in a cave
and wore garments which they wove
from animal skins.

It was the best time, they would learn to say.

WRITTEN IN CLAY

Homage to René Char

Half-reading some poems by René Char, in translation, I feel, nevertheless, as though I am touching something cold & hard. They strike me through my preoccupations, and I know they are real. I may be associating the poems with the little I know about René Char. But I feel, in my semi-abstracted state of mind, in which the poems are, however, almost physically present to me, that they are among the actions of a brave man's life. It is not only the aesthetic qualities that strike me, the coldness & the hardness, like precious stones in a mountain stream, but the sense of compacted meaning: words spoken, things made, from the matter of that life.

What I need to regain is a sense of the poem as a shaping action.

I have been inclined to pick up images like stones; but if a poem can be said to have a stone-like quality, that is because, like a stone, it has been shaped by powerful forces, which it 'contains'. Sometimes I think the materials will make the poem, or are the poem, so that it is only necessary to name them. And then, in this excessive reverence, what I starve is the mind – the mind that is fed by the matter of life, of felt or imagined experience, which it shapes . . .

Looking out through the library window I see rain falling straight down, lines of rain, from a heavy grey sky. It gathers in large dull-shining drops on the leaves of a hazel, which move slightly, shaking them off. Beyond the hazel, a large weeping beech – all the vegetation is dark, midsummer green – looks bowed down under the weight of the rain and the sky, and the naked boughs protruding through its depressed leafy crown are curved like arms raised in a forlorn defensive gesture. Beyond the beech the spire of the Nieuwe Kerk, delicately made for all its size, rises cleanly and neatly into the sky.

Outside the library, mind quieted by the poems and the rain, I really see the prehistoric pottery exhibited in a glass case. It stops me, rather than I decide to stop. On the bottom shelf there are urns, and one that I would call an eared pitcher, from the Late Bronze Age. On the top shelf, pots, beakers, bowls, all 'tableware', to be held in one hand, and a bowl about the size and shape of an ashtray standing on stubby legs, like a quaint animal. At a glance the pottery, which belongs to several cultures between 3400 BC and 2000 BC, looks dull in colour, though the shapes are immediately appealing. But at a second glance it reveals a warm orangy-red – a colour which at once makes me say the word 'fire-clay' to myself, though I don't actually know what it refers to – and marks appear, patterns of lines & strokes & small arrowheads, which might have been made with a fingernail or a microlith.

A notice refers to the artefacts as 'aardewerk uit de Late Steentijd', which looks as though it might be translated literally as 'earthwork out of the Late Stonetime' – a description closer to the common clay than 'pottery of the Late Stone Age'.

Looking at these things I touch them mentally, though they are out of reach of my hands. Their form and use invite touch – in that sense, they are like hands that reach out and touch me as I pass. It would be natural to handle them, and there would even be something inhuman about walking past with an indifferent glance.

As I cycle back, the rain soaks through my trousers at the knees and raises bubbles as it smacks hard into pools beside the road, and the smell of wet brick is suddenly sharper, the cycle paths bumpier and more abrasive under my tyres. Everything I have just seen and felt – the touch of the things – shapes itself in my mind as homage to René Char.

Fenrir

The terror slips from its dream image
along forest tracks and pathways of the mind,
and emerges scrawny,
exhausted by a long winter,
sniffing at the town garbage dump.

For now, the sun may complete
its nuclear explosions with impunity
out of the reach of slackened jaws.

On a portrait of Edith Södergran as a child

Nothing can stop it happening, Princess,
for already with your wondering
and frightened eyes you have chosen –
flash of gunfire over the frontier,
black flags at the sanatorium window:
a conscious dying – into life
that is shaped anew?
No one will prevent you, child,
from flying to the rooftops,
alone and eaglehearted – to look out,
to pluck the strings of a lyre
that stretch from roots of forest trees
to stars that take their fire
from the furnace burning in you –
pale and deep-sea creature,
magic child, woman whom no one knows.
Nothing will abort the birth
of a man-god, poet, or stifle song
within you, which you feed with blood.

A Picture-stone for Tomas Tranströmer

As the day darkens he travels north
sensing more than he can see
of pine forest, birches, lakes
where snow lies on the ice.

Boulders glimmer as the light fades.

★

Dance. Dance
to celebrate the kill.

Break the earth.

Whittle the wood
to a human shape
under the skull of heaven.

★

Odin mounts the trembling tree.

Christ crouches on the cross,
a foetus unwilling to be born.

★

Rune-stone, boat, axe-head.
So the land is made.

In the poem, too,
beauty and pain twisted
together violently
form an intricate design.

★

Islands, mountains, forests
descending to the shore,
opening on Baltic inlets.

He works with the place that made him.

He makes a mark on the blank side of the stone.

Edvard Munch: *The Sick Child*

Disease, insanity and death were the angels
which attended my cradle.

North is a dark green sea
which the boy shaking on the bed
was born to.
                    He is wrack
opening and shutting in the tide;
a ribbed shell dragged down
which waves knock
and the brine swills;

a mariner who will not drown.

                    Angels
attend him into the cold:

a woman the sea has broken on
bowing her down;
a girl with red hair, face
fragile as a moon
that floats out on the dark.

Remembering Berlin

In the park we found
an injured hooded crow
and you carried it back with us,
nursing it in your arms.

You walked beside me
asking insistently: 'Uncle,
how would you put this into words?'

Dear child,
did you really think
with your damaged brain
that I could?

                    What I saw
was so much injury
in body and mind,
in greedy fat fingers
of the healthy reaching
for our wallets or our sex.
I saw how tempting it is
to make History a god,
to fall down and adore.
'Lord, it is You
who have made us, You
who have shaped generations
and mould our lives.
There is not a particle,
not a cell that is free
to resist your Will.
The wide, straight roads
are yours, the blocks,
the parks, the city
inside the city, ghosts
of burning and ruined houses
behind the new façades.'

Remember the memorials,
the family gravestones
pockmarked with bullets,
the monumental buildings
of massive, grey stone –
shells of His power, more terrible
than the storms and furies
of ancient savage gods.

And the boy you regard lovingly
who sits on a park bench
with his back turned on the world
and feeds sparrows which land on his body
and eat from his hands.

Dust, grey soil, and on the top
of the man-made hill,
Teufelsberg,
a Space Age radar station;
below us the city lay
in every direction,
blocks, factories, towers,
pine woods where the wild boar
still runs free.
The hill itself was made
of rubble, burnt-out trams,
lorries, unimaginable things.

It was darker at Teufelsee,
and a few people were swimming
in water that was dark, and deep.
They were bodiless, white heads
moving over the surface.

Remember the mother who walks
up and down the street
from morning until night,
waiting for her son to come home
from the war.

Remember the man sitting
with his head framed
by the train window,
against a dusky red moon;
a tall man with a crippled foot,
a Slavic face; he was drunk
on vodka and talked at us
loudly, from some place
we had never visited.
The only words I knew were
'Atlantis', 'Einstein',
which he often repeated,
with total conviction,
offering us the key to the mystery.

We got the hooded crow back
alive, but had to kill it
to end its misery.

I only felt small;
and no, dear child,
I could not find the words.

Pictures of Bruges

1

The artist has painted St Luke
in the act of painting the Virgin
as she suckles the Child.
They are together in a room
that belongs to the artist's time –
richly but not lavishly furnished,
but a long way from the stable
and the beasts. Yet it seems that in this room
nothing matters except the space between
the painter and the woman and child,
which is the space of reverence and love.
Outside, a man and woman stand
with their backs to the house, looking
over a bridge, as burghers do,
at the water that carries their traffic.

They have all come a long way
to this moment, the artist,
St Luke, the mother and child,
the couple standing on the bridge.
There is nothing to suggest the light
in the room is not the same light
illuminating the water that flows away
through the city and into the world.

2

We arrived in the city towards dusk
and wandered as if in a dream
through medieval streets of gabled houses,
over bridges, beside quiet waterways,
by crucifixes and among gravestones,
in the light of expensive shop windows
and tourist cafés.
Everywhere, church spires towered above us.

I loved the place; it was a bridge
connecting water and stone,
the present and the past.
                    Here, in fading light,
shadow peopled the streets
with Hanseatic traders, Flemish artists,
peasants bringing in the produce of Flanders fields.
But already the dream was dying,
and I felt an unnatural chill,
an aching in my bones.

Then, in the shadow of a great church,
in a space near two Romanesque columns,
we stumbled upon a group of modern bronzes.
Four horsemen, mounted knights,
but under their armour they were fleshless,
skeletons,
except that each exposed an erect penis.
It was an impressive work –
which, suddenly,
made me feel sick with anger and disgust.

                              Did Christ die
that we should hate our flesh?
Are these his angels?
Pillars of Europe,
or maggots breeding in Europe's corpse?

I remembered the child's question,
after we had visited a monastery.
'If they believe God is light,
why do they live in darkness?'
It was dark now, except for the light
of shops and cafés,
as bells began striking together,
making another space.
But I could not forget the horsemen,
or the spirit that had wrought them,
and placed them here,
as if this were their centre,
the holy place where they belonged.

3

Stone walls,
argosies,
interiors with mirrors
displaying floors of patterned tiles,
books and paintings and tapestries,

and the faces look in
and the faces look out

4

The northern light reveals a world of faces
                                        and the faces
belong with the clothes.

Some have been cut from the same cloth.
Some are self-conscious,
ill at ease with their garments,
wondering who they are, asking.
There are proud faces, with cruel lines at the mouth,
a man with a hawk on his wrist
who is himself a hawk.

Among them all,
one body is naked,
wounded.

Verdun

In memory of Franz Marc

Thistles, poppies, blue cranesbill
by a dusty road.
In front, under the cloud stack
of an August sky,
                    the chalk ridge.

Trees, flowers, the earth
all showed me every year
more and more of their deformity.
I dream of a new Europe.

*

On a bluff a machine-gun post,
an iron mask with two eye-holes,
looks down on new growth.

Inside, the remains of a gun,
rusted and twisted.
The emptiness smells of fear.

The mask that blinded
has survived the face. It overlooks
slopes with harebells and young pines.

In spiritual matters new ideas
kill better than steel.

*

The blood throbs, pulses.
            This is the rhythm
in all things.

Deer feel the world as deer,
but whose landscape is this?

In the woods the war rages
with fiery signs.

All things, all creatures
are on fire. *All being*
is flaming suffering.

Under pine needles, the earth
that bled for purity
is matter,
                pulped and shattered.

In the immaculate cemetery
each white cross has a red rose
that smells sweet.

★

The Ossuary gleams
above trees and graves.

Whose temple is this?
                    Whose dream?

The tower is shaped
in the image of a shell
that blasted bodies to bits
but released the soul.

On the tower, the cross.

★

EN MEMOIRE DE FLEURY DEVANT DOUAMONT

She is Our Lady of Europe,
her chapel stands on rubble
under pines, on blasted,
cratered ground.

The woods are dark and still
where the village was,
but the chapel in a glade
is filled with sunlight.

A white butterfly wanders in
and flutters outside the porch
as though it, too, were in the picture.

*

New Year 1916. *The world*
is richer by the bloodiest war
of its many-thousand-year history.

And all for nothing.

Towards Arras

From Picardy and the land of the Somme
the late summer sky had lowered,
become a roof of dark blue cloud.
And it broke in downpour, shattering
on roadside memorials and regiments of graves,
smoking across the fields,
the mounds and ditches, that already,
after seventy years, look prehistoric.
And as we drove towards Arras,
slowly, against the pounding
and blinding cloudburst,
I thought of Edward Thomas
and how he would have loved
the violence of this passing storm.

The Stones of Brittany

Most of them dwarf us

                                        the menhir
shaped like a giant phallus
that has fallen and broken

                                        the passage,
symbols carved in granite,
a fine axe
which might also be a plough
furrowing the stone

                                        the alignments
which could swallow a multitude

the one I return to
is a broken circle,
stones on the shore
of an island of megaliths,
stones in the water
gulls and cormorants
perched on their heads,
which the tide covers
and withdraws to reveal
again
                                        the circle

wave-shaped curves of the beach,
the curves of the windrows
of dark brown wrack,
earth wheeling
                                        the turning sky

Hieratic Head of Ezra Pound

Scholars will speak of vision,
even, without irony, 'the final vision'.

The mind of Europe
founders among its ruins.

Words must fail.

The man looks up. The light of the stockade
glares in his eyes.
He is guarded, and displayed.

There is no shadow for him here,
unless it is memory
peopled with shades:

                    Gaudier
in his studio under the railway arch,
a man of the renaissance,
the air between them alive with ideas.
They dispose of an age of statues,
a trash of books.
The poet is quick to give.
The sculptor works on the marble,
winning every inch
'at the point of the chisel'.

Naturally, the sculpture
will survive the carver,
and outlast the model.
It will gaze back down the century,
over the work of other men of order
whose material is flesh and blood and bone.

The Head looks impassively over the ruins.
The poet looks out
towards the mountain, beyond the Pisan cage.

Two Figures from Catalonia

1

They called him Bes, he was a god
brought over by the Phoenicians.
A gross, flabby figure,
a cross between a wrestler
and a dissolute Buddha
with a worn, distorted face.

                    We can't tell
what he meant once,
but he retains some power
                    he makes us smile.

2

She too is time-worn
but her beauty is palpable,
desirable.
                It is not
that she might have risen from the sea
yesterday
with the mucous glisten of birth
still wet on her skin.
                              She belongs
among the dusty paths, stone walls,
holes in the ground
and to the hot sun, and dark
eternal flames of cypresses.
            She is Aphrodite
in whose beauty
desire calls to desire
making, unmaking, the bonds of time.

Ode to Antonio Gaudí

When I first saw
the façade of the Nativity
I laughed, and wanted to cry
and the imp in me itched to say
to the imp in him, 'So this
is what can happen
when parents let little boys
play with sand!'

But it was not like the work
of that other devout man,
Gerald of Wales,
who built cathedrals
in the sand at Tenby,
and grew up to be a bishop.

This was about play
more than power,
and more than both,
and as well as both,
it was about wonder,
Gaudí's, and the wonder
of the people (myself
among them) who stood
amused, intrigued,
amazed, and first and most
of all, wondering.

This was about being a man
who was a great artist
and a child, who made
a thing that stands, and flows,
and seems to melt and run
and drip, like water
or forms that grow in water
and embody its rhythms
and its shapes.

The work of a man
who knew the Adoration
of the Serpent and the Beast;
who had seen angels riding
the winds on wineskins;
St Michael with wings
made of peacock feathers,
slaying a monster that lies
on its back exposing
an orange belly, like a newt's.
This man's familiar was
John the Baptist, wide-eyed,
brown-bearded, standing
in a desert of cacti
that leap about him like green flames.

And their makers, the makers
of these images, were his people,
the people he belonged to,
with whom, at another time,
he had embroidered
the Tapestry of Creation
using the umbrella pines,
the Catalan soil and fields
for materials and tools.

Gaudí of Barcelona,
the city that gave him freedom
to embody such a vision
and most deserves his blessing.

He died, the great work
unfinished,
and because of that
more natural, more
a place to play in,
and laugh and cry
and wonder at the maker,
man-child, and his praise
in the body of Creation
that begins and has no end.

The Mother of Laussel

You may know her by the rock
she is made of, and the scars
of the ice.

She is the one who nurtured the bison,
and starved it,
and holds aloft its horn,
which is also her symbol,
the crescent moon.

She is without a face.
Is she, then, Goddess of Love?

Examine the deep breasts,
the bulging thighs,
the curve of her belly.
With her free hand
she points down, between her legs.

She stands at the cave-mouth
and is herself the cave.
This is the birthplace
of the rock rose and the sabre-tooth.

You will recognise her
by a touch, when, for the last time,
you kiss the cold brow-bone
of the woman who bore you.

CROSSWAYS

Tel Gezer

And Solomon built Gezer.

How simple the words that have only
one meaning – blood.

1

I wanted to ask you, Shimshon,
after that day when we worked together
in the fields, breaking the stony soil
and planting young olive trees,
when blisters wept on my hands
and the sunflowers in the heat
seemed also to turn their faces
to talk to each other, as you to me.
That day, Shimshon, black Hebrew,
soldier and lover of trees,
just man, but fierce and strong
in defence of your people, you
told me the history under our feet,
in the kibbutz and the Tel rising
above us as we worked, hacking out
thistles and tough-rooted fennel,
making room for the young olives.
And at night, as I lay in bed
with aching body, between sleep
and waking, images blazed,
or fell dully like drops of blood,
and voices crossed in my head.
My friend, I wanted to ask you
the meaning of the words.

2

A language of soil,
cracked and brown,
with a look of old parchment.
Fields of sunflowers.
Then pine trees and limestone boulders
as the hill climbs.

A path to tread carefully,
dry and pitted,
where red ants swarm
carrying seed-heads.
Caves. A prickly pear cactus.
Concrete floors hidden in grass,
a spent cartridge among stones.

In the heat, the Tel is alive
with insects and birds. A tortoise
rustles dead thistles, regards
the intruder with a black eye.
On the great mound, a row
of standing stones. And five storks,
which fly off under a moon
like a partly blown dandelion clock.

Has history burnt out history
in this place, and left nothing?

Image throws down image,
word shatters word
in the silence.

The cracked earth gapes
with dusty mouths.

Land in the heart
of an Arab poet in Paris,
who looks through boulevards
at a stone village
with vineyards and olives.

Land in the heart
of a Jew staring
through the walls of Europe
at bare, waiting earth,
sun like honey on the stone.

3

From a deep cleft on the Tel,
a hawk flies out of the ground
and sheers off, circling, wind-ruffled.
Grassblades quiver under it.
And here the hawk has preyed since
before Pharaoh destroyed Gezer
and Solomon rebuilt it of mud
and stone, or the Assyrians
perfected the art of exile; since
long before the kibbutz formed
a small, green pool below,
in the dustbowl of stony hills.

Tel Gezer: where the road
from Egypt to Syria
crosses the road from Jaffa
to Amman, with the Mediterranean
a long, bright sliver in the west.
Mount of Temptation for a people
with everything to lose,
and a people with nothing;
who look down on the valley of Aijalon
where the moon stood still,
and Latrun, the House of the Good Thief,
and over the hard hills of Judea
towards Emmaus on the road to Jerusalem.
Each name in this place is a sound
of approaching thunder – it would hollow
the skull with a blast of fire
to see what it means.

Tel Gezer at the crossways:
destination of roads
from Warsaw and Buchenwald;
exodus of Arabs from Abu-Shusha
and El-Biryeh and El-Kubab,
on the road to refugee camps,
kicking up the dust of Palestine.

4

Pharaoh has gone up and taken Gezer
and burnt it with fire.
He has overrun the perimeter
and slain the Canaanites.
Nomad falls on nomad
for the olives and vineyards
and stony ridges, for a dream
that flows with the hills
and settles in green valleys –
that the wolf lie down with the lamb
and a little child lead them.

Captives scratch their hatred on the rocks.
A curse on Simeon, may fire descend
from heaven and devour his house.
A curse on the Christians.
A curse on Saladin and the heathen.

A curse on the Jews –
our hills speak it, and the mouths
of dynamited wells,
the rock speaks for us,
and the silence and the red wind
that blows from the desert
and every crack in the soil.
There is no bare earth –
each stone has sucked up blood
and memory inscribes the dust.

Our memory – and now we are afraid
to appear in our fields.
Let the Jews seek their friend
where he lies sightless on the Tel
and a tortoise eyes him curiously.

And Yusif lies buried
in the rubble of his home.

5

The young orchard demands our care.
We go out with rifles, one eye
on the work, the other on the rocks.

What calls?
A bee-eater, brilliant blue and green.
At a touch each rock may stun and blind.

Will the golden fields wait in vain
for the combines?
Will Arab hatred silence the harvest?
We have put sweat into this land.
We had nothing – the very name
of Man cut from our foreheads.
And now hold a home, a camp
among enemies, a foundation stone
of the State.

Summer comes, fruit ripens, swallows
high in the blue are small as bees.
An army comes out of the hills.

They cross the perimeter with tanks,
circling, driving us in.
First the stable is hit, then
the fuel-tank; hay-sheds blaze
and the air is thick with smoke
and stench. What does it mean?
You know the bodies are comrades
you won't see any more, and no one
will replace you if you fall.

At night we counter-attack: no one,
only a few Arabs looting the rubble,
scattering feathers from quilts
and pillows to the wind.
They melt away into the orchard
and through their empty village streets.
They vanish into the hills.

6

A pine marten moves sinuously,
with alert head, over the grass
and by the cypresses, past
the Hebrew graves.
At the foot of the Tel, a wall of names –
people from ghetto and death-camp
who came here to make a home
from bare earth, and died together
on a day in June when the harvest
was waiting in the fields. And now,
at the start of a new day, Shimshon
drives out a tractor, and Jewish children
crowd round him, their hero and friend.
No snipers, no ambush today
among the huge limestone boulders
and fortified caves. No detail
sent to eliminate neighbours.
A bee-eater calls, alighting on
Solomon's mud wall, and lizards,
dragon-headed, look over the edge
at red ants swarming on the path
and rusted tank tracks lying in a tangle
of herbs and passion flowers and barbed wire.
Now it is a place of swallowtails,
of hawk and eagle, and the storks
on their flight from Africa to the Elbe.

From the kibbutz and Hebrew cemetery
the path climbs to Abu-Shusha –
but there is nothing left, only
potsherds and bits of white mosaic
sprinkled with dust.
There are moshaves on the sites
of El-Biryeh and El-Kubab.
Opposite the Tel, looking down
to Aijalon and Latrun and the road
to Jerusalem, a new village,
and Arabs working in a vineyard.

Below the site of the orchard,
where the border used to run,
sunflowers shimmer in the heat.
They pulsate, full-faced, or hang
dried heads, heavy with seed.
Bees yellow with pollen climb out
and lumber away through the air.
The flowers seem to dance when
the wind stirs, then turn to each other
in a golden, silent conversation.

The young olives stand in the sun.

Will they grow thick with fruit?

Who will harvest them?

Jerusalem sketchbook

Dust, grey dust,
a valley of graves
below the Gate of Mercy.

An old Arab leading a donkey
laden with toilet rolls down
the track past Absalom's Tomb.

*

A display of olives and roses.

Across the road broken glass
crowns the high wall of a garden.
Through a locked iron gate we see
a sign nailed to a tree
announcing the betrayal.

*

Olives, of course. And cypresses.
And waste ground littered with bottles,
rusted iron, oil drums.
A carrion crow picking over it.

But don't forget the cock standing
on an old bed in an orchard.
Or the donkey too bored to look at us,
lying flat out in a pool of dust.

*

Sleeping in the city sky
among TV aerials and goats
and clusters of conical
stone roofs,

I am woken at 4 a.m.
by *what*!

From a minaret close by –
echoes
over the city
rise and fall
answering –

melancholy,
beautiful –

song of a world different
from everything I know.

★

Did we pay 200 shekels to see
a tub of grey sand
full of candle ends
or the imprint of Christ's foot?

★

Black beards. Black clothes.
The men striding together
down the middle of the road
are a people apart who brush
all who are not themselves
into the shadows.

Arabs merge with the shadows,
emerge from the stones.

★

Morning. A procession
in the street.

At the centre,
held on the shoulders of bearers,
an open coffin.

Looking back at us,
a dead man's face.

★

Among Arab women stepping
with bundles on their heads
or squatting with baskets
at the Damascus Gate,

among tourists and soldiers
and Arab boys on donkeys,

Behold: the new world –
an American evangelist
wild in a red shirt.

He holds a black case
with 'Elijah' written on one side,
and on the other
'Try Jesus By Faith'.

★

The poet describes his city
to us, affectionately.
He calls it 'a big bad poem'.

★

So this is where flesh
oozes spirit.

Wrung in the press,
out of the reek,

you see this:

drops like dark juice
on the Via Dolorosa,
dashed in the dust.

Jericho

1

Oasis of flowers and fruit,
green in the wilderness:

hibiscus and bougainvillaea
among date-palms, red
acacia sheltering houses,
lemons and oranges in the streets.

No reason here for a man
to renounce the world,
who builds a winter palace
by the Mountain of Temptation,
with all good things that water
and wealth provide –

a dancing floor, courtyards
and shady chambers, a mosaic
cool under his feet –
the Tree of Life,
full of leaves and heavy with fruit,
flanked by a lion
leaping on a gazelle.

2

Hard and dry under the sun,
Old Jericho is a stairway
into the ground, down through
mud-brick and beaten clay,
walls tumbled on walls,
tower on tower, down
through debris choking the way –
and no moist tongue, nothing
but a clay tablet to speak
for thousands of years.

At the bottom of it all,
the floor on which hunters
made a camp and raised a shrine
by a spring watering the desert.

3

That none should be lost –

all things speak against it:
the sandgrains that want
only to be forgotten,
buried in the sandhills;
the water that flows,
moulding all to its nature;
the powers that go down
stroke on stroke, butchering
or being butchered
for Mammon or for God.

He who knows their names
and those of their children
and of their families, may he
inscribe them in the book of life.

Bethlehem

Over all, suddenly, with a crash
that sends sheep scrabbling
at stone walls or squirming in the dust,
a jet fighter crosses the target area.

Over David's fields and the trunks
of felled olive trees, two thousand
years of life compacted, swirling
in the wood. Over stony fields,
hard, white hills and Herod's
mountain tomb crowning the wilderness.

All look up blindly –
women from weeping at Rachel's Tomb,
soldiers at roof-top gunposts,
Arabs selling fruit in Manger Square
or at lathes turning out holy figures,
a tourist enjoying the ironies,
who remembers another place:
starlight on the home fields,
voices drawing closer from door to door.

O little town

*

They will sing a new song
descending from the fields
of galactic dust,
from the black cold
by the blaze of nuclear suns.

They will come down
out of the nebulous dark
to the ruined stable,
gas shell and shattered atom
lighting the night they blindly stare at

*

And so we enter
under an old doorway
made to keep out animals,
and descend through histories:

between pillars stained brown
as old canvases, under
ikons and a brass hanging lamp
balancing a tzar's crown,
past symbols, past stonework
of Crusaders, Armenians, Greeks.

Under the gaze of Elijah
over the long falls of his beard
we come to the mosaic floor
and the floor below the floors,
down to the simple place
all has been built to protect,
or bury . . .
when, suddenly, with a crash
that shakes the walls,
a jet fighter crosses the hills

and we stand with candles
shaking in our hands

*

Lantern light on faces
under the shadowy cross-beams.

So the scene is set:

Mary wrapped in a night-sky cloak.
Ox and ass, big-eyed, nuzzling
into the cradle.
Joseph leans head on hand, resigned
to what he loves but does not understand

*

A smouldering warmth,
fire in the dead of the year,
a red glow at the heart
of black cold, and starlight
falling through the broken roof,
a smell of hay,

the child's cry among the farthest stars

Walking to Capernaum

1

Such violence struck here –
a new thing, a word with power:

And thou, Capernaum,
which art exalted unto heaven,
shalt be brought down to hell.

A gentler word
where the sea laps the shore:
The damsel is not dead, but sleepeth.

2

What I feel most is the heat,
and sick at the unreality
of bad art:

a sloppy English poem
which someone has fixed on a wall
at the site of the miracle
of loaves and fishes;

new stained glass daubing
the interior of the chapel built
over the rock where Christ
is said to have said to Peter . . .

Compared to these,
I could love the wooden donkeys
and camels and holy families
from the factory at Bethlehem.

Unreal, in a sweat of heat
and bad blood, I dip
my seamy face in the water.

It tastes of salt, and is
a dull silvery blue
on a day of desert cloud.

A crane – not, thank God,
a symbol – but a white crane,
with long, wispy hairs at the back
of its neck, stands
fishing in the shallows.
A black lizard looks at me
over the edge of a black stone.

3

On the road between
orchards and tomato fields;
in the dust thrown up
by tourist coaches;
between the columns
and among pine needles lying
on the ruins of Peter's house,
I try to imagine them:

The girl waking surprised
with hunger in her eyes;
the woman cured by a touch;
that loud cry, the man
on the floor of the synagogue –
torn and empty, but clean.

What had he seen? What thing
had cried with his voice?

And the fishermen
as they put out –
from this moment, no
denial will swerve their aim.

The port they left behind
is a heap of black stone.

4

It is evening, and very still;
heavy cloud, the colour
of smouldering ash,
obscures a misshapen moon.
Tiny fish swarm blackly
on the surface, nudging
crusts from our seafront café,

Suddenly, the wind rises. Trees
sway and open, lights go out
and napkins soar into the air;
waiters leap to catch bottles
and glasses blown off the tables.
A cloud swirls through the streets
and covers our plates with sand.
At once the sea heaves up
a huge, slippery shoulder
against the wall.

In the sudden violence
I see them for the first time:
the small port waiting, still
waiting – nets spread on the wall,
barrels of salt fish on the quay –
and the men who will not return,
but are borne up at a word
as their ship drives through the storm.

MOTHERLAND

Homer Dictating

for Gerard Casey

It is the body that speaks
and what it speaks of is the man
and his suffering, his thought,
the vision he sees in his blindness.

His hands speak,
and his mouth speaks more than words,
and his whole body,
an old man's but still powerful.

In the depths behind his eyes
warriors boast on the windy field,
Odysseus adventures on the seas,
among magical and dangerous islands,
and strains his eyes against the light
and sting of spray to catch a wisp of smoke
far off, rising from the hearth-fires of Ithaca.

Rembrandt's Homer is a man,
but the light of the sacred
is upon him –
a pale watery gold
falling across his shoulders and his face.
But it does not shine from afar,
from another world.
The sacred is part of him,
dwelling in light and shadow,
and his body is the landscape of his soul.

For the painter has taken clay in his hands,
common clay,
and shaped from it the image, God-given,
which he knew in his own world,
among merchants and soldiers,
Rabbis and adventurers,
the grand and the poor of Leiden
and Amsterdam, and knew
most intimately in his own flesh,
in the imagination that is breath and blood and spirit.

With this he saw, and humbled his seeing
to know the vision of the blind,
of Homer dictating,
with sightless eyes,
the seer of men and women and gods.

Steadily the day burns

Bees hum, yellow and black,
diving deep into whorls
of Jerusalem Sage.

A dog barks, a billy goat
strains at his rope,
and there it is –

the Byzantine church standing
in the fields, inside
the circle of mountains.

Within, the dome is blue
as a thrush's egg,
with openings on the sky.

Could Heaven be lighter
or more like air?

We look down, we see
dusty glass covering
a case set in the floor,
and through it, dimly,
a heap of bones.
They look to me like sticks
gathered to start a fire.

How unhuman the faces
of the mountains!

                                        The dome
shows in its curves
the shape of a hand.

Steadily the day burns
round it with a blue flame.

Panagia Kara

Our Lady the Virgin,
white-washed among cypresses,
where the shadows bear fruit
and the familiar becomes strange:

a rich darkness,
a painted cave,
but not where Zeus was born,
or Kronos slobbered,
swallowing a swaddled stone.
Serene, accepting, this Christ
is stronger than the savage gods.

Cool, pictured shadows –
green & red, orange & brown –
show the Nativity. Herod's massacre.
Grapes and lemons grow,
birds sing,
on branches of Paradise.

On the table of the Last Supper
a wonderful fish –
surely a red mullet –
looks at us, and winks.

Yet for all its pictures
Crete is a script I cannot read.
At Lato, high on a mountain ridge,
the empty arena waits.
Golden brown hornets fly
heavy with purpose through
stillness and heat.
Old men and women dressed in black
reap barley by hand in small,
yellow fields, a donkey
stands waiting in an olive's shade.

Seeing an old woman gathering herbs,
a shepherd asleep on a bank, sheep
grazing around him and the sun shining
on his bald head,
I see how little I have seen,
how much I have that weighs me down.

Palikare

Later we will see him –
his lean, strong, stone-carved face –
but today we see,
on the ascent,
hooded crows
and what might be eagles,
three big birds, just glimpsed,
circling a crag.
There are lemons,
oranges, silver-leaved olives,
white anemones;
even here,
in mist on the heights,
the horn of plenty.
But we will not remember them
as we remember the skulls,
the glass cases
filled with skulls.

It is Easter,
the church is prepared,
with lilies,
it is time to think of courage
and death.
This is the place.

I can hardly credit it,
even here, in a country
where courage is common as rock,
and grows from it
hard face
to hard face.
To destroy
your people, your kind –
men, women, children –
and destroy
the enemy, who otherwise
will defeat you
and take all you have.

To die together
in one blast,
friend, enemy,
stripped of the names,
lying together,
skulls
that are indistinguishable
one from another, but not to you
who know them
absolutely
at the last moment
that never ends,
each
a living soul.

You recognise them,
every one.
You bring them, shepherd
to the pastures,
the green fields
of the dead.

I have heard of courage, Palikare,
but it would be a lie
to say I understand.

Later I will see you,
your lean, strong face
carved in stone.

Europa

for Lindsay and Phoebe Clare Clarke

The sun stands naked
out of the shade, in a space
of poppies and fig-trees,
                    an empty space
where Greeks and Romans
built their worlds.

                         Over all
the breath of the bull-god,
the sear of lightning that burned
a blackness into the light.

What havoc it caused –
columns, sarcophagi,
a headless female statue,
the dome of St Titus,
                    emptied,
filled with flutterings
of sparrows.
                    And a side chapel
where the faithful and the sick
bring medicine bottles,
prayers for healing,
ikons of the Virgin,
and I placed a bunch of grass
in memory of a dead poet, a woman
who knew the value of such things.

*

What did he know
the Philosopher of Gortyn?

Here he is a peripatetic
among Pans and Roman nobles,
a man with a fine beard
and sandalled feet,
a museum piece
that is almost whole.

What idea? What salve
for the wound between us,
the emptiness, the worlds
vanished into the ground?

*

Once, they say,
Earth was a giant pithos
pouring out oil and wine
embracing the dead.
                                        No war troubled
the forests and mountains
or bloodied the inshore water –
nets of sunlight and foam.

Then the air darkened
with the flight of the god.
She clung unwillingly to his back,
fingers wound tight among curls,
that moments before had plucked flowers
where she walked by the shore.
And so, with the waves
still swimming in her eyes,
she was laid down and the bull
hung over her, a cloudy mass,
                      and bore her down.

It was here, under the plane tree,
where the stream runs
and the water is living,
                      never so living,
under the naked sun.

EARTH SONG CYCLE

Women dancing in a field of poppies

Slowly at first they measure
their steps as the sun strengthens,
the poppies flame redder,
the sea-blue deepens, and they,
women in white, loose-limbed,
flowing, circle hand in hand,
turn faster, and faster,
leap and fly till their feet
are birds, white birds, skimming.
And round they go, wing to wing,
as the field revolves and the sea,
and earth veils and unveils,
white and blue, under their heels,
which skim and pause and come to rest
while round and round them turns
the scarlet field,
                                        and O the earth.

She descends into the dark

For now she knows nothing
but terror, rage.
                                        And what she throws off
is the scent of it, the reach
of the stamens that beckoned,
the face of the flower
that drew her in, and closed,
as a sundew swallows a fly.

                      Beyond this,
the meadow spins in her mind.
She feels on her hands the hands
of her friends, gripping,
torn away.
                      It is a lost world
she sees in the dark
and nothing more, not the god
whose sweat she smells
and breath she feels on her face
as he drives her down.

                      Later she will see,
but now there is only his breath
mixed with the reek of horses,
the smell of roots
and engulfing earth.

How can she know what visions
will be born of her story,
or even if it is true?
There is, perhaps, no power
but hers, no god to command.

This is not the moment to see,
nor the moment of those
who will follow, seeking her
under the ground.
                      How many will come
as the light fails, or the glare
extinguishes sight.
                           How many
will plead with her
for annihilation
or beg to return.
                          Only now
the dark has taken her
and she has left, to her friends
reeling apart in the meadow,
and her mother, listening
to the echo,
                      only a cry.

And every cleft is mute

A cry echoes among the mountains.

                    Somewhere
the earth has opened. Where?
Where is her daughter?

She searches and searches
but finds no sign.

Who cares? Not the god
who leaps and dives and plunges
to death in ecstasy
and forms again among the foam.

Not the stones she kicks over,
or the cuttle-bones
or globs of tar.

Not the roots she finds
sodden with salt –
            images
that would bewitch her,
grotesques
with human form.

Are these, maybe, a sign?
She calls again
and no one answers.

The sea changes.
It is clouded glass,
into which she looks, and sees
nothing.

No one. Every cleft
is closed against her call.
She sets her bleeding feet
on shells, weed, foam.

Turning over, the waves
are cavernous,
smooth for an instant
and full of sand.
                                        Light rides in
on crest and underlip.

The day will be immaculate,
the night perfect, that sees
her torch wandering in blackness
like a moon.

She hides her golden hair

Let him bellow,
                                        the thunderer
wrapped in cloud,
for this, she says,
is only the beginning.

                    Birds
returning to her without a message
drop dead from the sky,
snail shells bleach in heaps
spiralling down to dust,
snake and green lizard
crawl into holes to die.

And she hides her hair
in a hood.
                         As a stormcloud
falls on the harvest,
blackness blots out the gold.

                         She walks alone
among her people, searching
their sightless eyes
for a sign.
                         No one answers
when she calls and calls.

Men break picks on the fields,
oxen strain to shift the plough,
seeds fall on soil turned to stone.

She will waste all
as she is wasted,
calling and calling.

Ovens and storage bins,
the giant pithoi
that poured out bounty,
all their round bellies
hold emptiness and mould.

And this, she says,
is only the beginning.

Afterwards
the fall of ash,
seas white with corpses,
no swellings on earth
but the bloated dead.

Let him look down
on his handiwork,
thunderer,
father of desolation.

Who will survive
to make an offering
or give him thanks,
when she, who brings
all things in their seasons,
provides nothing,
and no one but the dead?

A hymn to Demeter

Pardon us
that we will
our end & forgive

the poet
his ambition
to stand alone

on a high peak
surveying
the waste.

Take the map
from our hands
which we take
for the world

& let us be
where earth
and waters meet

& make, for you,
a song.

'Christ is risen!'

Again the priest
has cried aloud
in a joyful voice
to the people
who move off together
carrying candles,
a procession
of white moons
threading the dark.

Once more a cry
sounds where a cry
has echoed
over corn field
and olive grove
across thousands
of years. Again
the cave stands open
and the faithful see.

Written in clay

What could he do, the swineherd
gaping at the meadow?
                                        Had he dreamed
the earth had opened, closed,
his herd gone squealing down
along with her,
                              the fairest flower?

What could he do but wait,
and learn, maybe, that flowers spring
from rotting flesh.

*

She will come back (they said),
the sweet, red seed is on her tongue,
she will rcturn
and we will taste her words

                        And when she rose,
she will descend (they said)
she will descend again,
and rise
                there is no end,
spring air returns,

the birds repeat their calls,
the wind of winter wails
in trees and round the house
the same old song

no end

no end

★

He looked (the squeal
still ringing in his ears)
and every thing
everywhere
spoke to him of her

She was the water and the fish,
the stream within the stream
becoming flesh,
she was the black grain and the bread,
the wet clay and the pot,
the light, the dark,
the silence and the word,
she was all formless
on the verge of form, and form
becoming formlessness.

And so he tasted on his tongue
the song
and sang it to a lute
made from his flesh and bone

and wrote it in the clay

no end

no end

IMAGINING WALES

Guests of Silence

1. *Images made and unmade by the River Wye above Tintern*

Sheer above the river, cliffs.
Stroke upon stroke the current
cleaves rock.
Water builds as it breaks.
Tall above cliffs, trees.

Wrinkled like the mother
first imagined in stone,
an ancient face that is not
for one moment the same.

Now it looks up
and is eaten away: a gargoyle
made of water, spouting.
Vortex. Whirl of galaxies.
Circle on circle
shatters and shapes.

            Ripple,
dint in armour
of black-bright scales.
Mailed crusaders lie in the long bed
silvery-dark.
History is a shadow roughing
the smooth skin.
Bubbles of air and light.

Glaciers crawl down the valley.
Lava erupts through a crack in the earth
and bears down, down.

The river is full
and still has room for the sky.

Lines and nets of grass
hang tangled from branches.
And the river is itself a tree

growing along the ground,
bark-ridged,
feeding with millions of leaves.

Cold, winter-blue.
Alder-green under floodmarks.
Mud colours, a sheen
of red earth.

Suddenly
a coin of light
minted this moment,
a stroke of shadow.

So the world's likeness
appears on the canvas,
and washes out.

Crumbled and carried down,
the red earth is Adam's clay.
A wallowing mudbank
is the beached ark.

The water-face waits
desolate
for the shadow of the dove.

Such bareness
water is, a truth
too slippery-quick to grasp,
skin-taut and bodiless
spirit, and to the poet
who comes despairing of his mind
a companion
that murmurs of the source
and infant spring,
and flows with him, and is his life.

The river fattens the lowlands
with silt, gurgles
to plainchant, whispers

under aisles raised on green lees
to the god of light.

                    Such sad music
the human ear shapes,
hearing in the one flow
sighs of a multitude
falling one by one.

Otter and water-rat dive,
shaped to rhythms that slip
the word-knot,
the quaver.

                    So bare,
yet utter.
Channel of word and song.

Water from mountain-
mother of rivers,
fleet daughter,
breaker and builder
of the parent ground.

Sweet-salt self
cleaving and raising,
sheer below cliffs
stroke on stroke
the river is

2. *At the Polish Scout House, St Briavels*

The house on the hillside
looks into Wales. It is fragile,
a matchwood ark, between
the beech woods and the Wye.

Yet it is we who are shapes
of air through which leaves drift
and the river runs; guests
of the silence our noise does not break.

In her shrine
the Virgin prays for her people.
She remembers Monte Cassino
and the Polish dead. At her back
autumn in the English woods smells
sweet. Leafmould heaps up
on the coverts of Katyn.

What hides from us in rooms
painted with her colour,
blue as the November sky?
Our feet brush floors rubbed bare
by the tread of regiments; heroes
whose names we cannot pronounce
look down on us from the walls.
Silence lives in the rooms we fill
with emptiness, where we drift
leaf-light in a current of air.

3. *Tintern Abbey: the white wind*

Brother, did you too know
the white wind, the sudden
violent wind that streams
downriver from the hills?

Or did you at holy office hear
a sigh, a sound of wings, a song
at one with the song of love?
Or see Christ's dear blood
stream in the stained glass
where now the wind drives through?

Would we know each other
soul to soul, you who knelt
at Calvary, world's centre
within these walls, and I
who stand in the dirt nave
open to the sky?
I do not think so – only now

I feel close to you, under
the white wind from the hills
which blasts cold and downpour
through the shell, the ruin
raised on all that is broken,
the house that is always to build.

Variations on a theme by Waldo Williams

Beth yw gwladgarwch? Cadw ty
Mewn cwmwl tystion.
('What is love of country? Keeping house
amid a cloud of witnesses.')

1. *Bryniau Presely*

for Susan and Huw Jones

Fire was first,
surging out of the earth.
Then the flux,
the molten stream
cooling.

And the stone stood,
intruding,
weathering.

On Carn Meini
it spoke to them:
blue stone,
sacred to the earth
and the fire within the earth.

Manhandled,
shaped, hauled by water
and dragged over land,
lifted up,
the stones stand,

circles,
silent tongues.

*

Or say it was by sea
the pattern was woven – skin boats
navigating along sea-boards
that would be known one day
as Brittany and Cornwall,
Ireland and Wales,
drawing together the stones,
tracing the loops and knots
of an intricate design.

It was by way of a long haul
and the energy that creates
the stone circle,
the upland pasture,
language that knits the kin,
and over all,
deeper than the sky,
durable as rock,
the invisible roof and walls.

How long does it take,
how many thousands of years,
to prepare the eternal moment?

On a day when the curlew returns,
its cry circling the moor,
suddenly, to the man
in love with time, the whole land
is the poem he will never write,
birth cry, love song, threnody
woven in voices of the living
and voices of the dead.

*

The history that he reads
is written in the land.
Its words are:
                capstone
                ogham
                Celtic cross.

Its syntax is the serpent
of the river coiling
between walls of rock.
It is homely; it moves
between neighbours
working in the fields,
in their silence, in their talk.

The history that he reads
is written in the sky:
warplanes; marks
of a slavery that imprisons him,
a man who is free.

*

Loss, surely, is part of it,
loss and despair.

Does he think sometimes
that the building is finished:
a labyrinth that no one can enter,
a house of the dead?

Or does he feel
the touch of dead hands
on monolith or carved cross?
Or hear in the silence
voices that speak of their time,
their loss?

Already the new ground crumbles,
shifts under foot –
the bishop's palace, empty as a cromlech,
the cathedral, shaken by a sonic boom.

The story is not finished,
and will not be, unless
metaphors cease to carry meaning,
the fountains of symbol run dry.

It is still the eighth day
where he walks on the hills,
a witness among witnesses,
a maker among carpenters of song.

*

Often I walked on Mynydd Bach
among the ruined hearthstones
and looked north towards the mountains,
south to distant Presely.

Mist would fall suddenly,
I would not know where I was
or be certain of climbing down
where I wanted to be.

Once I stood still
and let the mist soak me
until it cleared,
a whiteness dissolving
from new earth, washed sky,
wispy spirits departing,
vanishing like faces we know
better than we know our own.

*

As for the dead
we may talk of them
but how shall we know them
until they are people we love?

Then they belong to us,
and we belong with them.

There is nowhere to fall,
the land under our feet is whole.

*

On Windmill Hill
the ditches are filled
with split animal bones,
flint tools, sherds.

They may be sacrifices,
or refuse.
No one know why they are there.

Into the mystery, walking
among the remains,
the poet comes.
He sees the skeleton of a girl
who died thousands of years ago,
and she touches him,
she opens his eyes.

He sees, and what he sees
touches us; we are more alive
in the open place:
the great house
with invisible roof and walls.

2. *Ebbw Vale*

for Lee Grandjean

1

Tongues of fire
that transformed the earth,
that joined it in iron circuits –
what have they left?

Three ponies graze
on a green field
above the valley.

These, and an old post
with strands of rusted wire,
keep out despair.

2

If there are spirits
they are like the trees
on the mountainsides
whose shape is the struggle to grow.

Iron did not master them.
Still they burn, over the seared
and dross-hard ground:

shocks of black, windblown flame.

3

What word will you carve
to speak for the dead
and not dishonour them
who forged a new world in the heart?

If there are sounds
they are valley voices,
twined with the turns of the wind
and the falling stream.

When silence fell
on the last hammer-blow,
what remained in the air
but a strand of their song?

4

If there are witnesses
the wind blows through their mouths,
rain pricks their eyes
as it dints the mountain pond
which was once a mine.

And around them weathers circle,
as the high buzzard turns,
drifts and falls,
and the far ridge crumbles away.

5

What do they see but defeat?

Eyes that have watched so long
see violence woven with hope.

When all has been blown away
what lasts is a twisted flame.

3. *Strata Florida (1)*

for Wynn Thomas

They did not believe in the world
yet they built one, drawing a line
from the centre to the margins:
from Citeaux and the vineyards of Burgundy
to the Welsh uplands.

Rhys Prince of Wales granted them land:
champaign, arable, mountain pasture,
for the cure of his soul
and the souls of those before him
and the souls of those still to be born.

They expected the world to end,
and it did, not once but several times –
by fire, by dissolution.

At last almost nothing remained
of the visible structure –
stubs of walls, foundations,
a doorway open on clouds, hills.

On the surface, there is little
to speak of the makers – monks,
abbots who were patrons of poets,
princes who set aside the sword,
lay brothers who cut down woods,
built roads, tended flocks of sheep.

Only bare tombstones,
and slabs carved with a cross,
fragments of knotwork:
relics of the great design.

And near the yew that was full-grown
six hundred years ago
when a fellow poet honoured him,
Dafydd ap Gwilym lies.
Old then, the yew is ancient now,
hollow, but still alive –
no ruin, Dafydd's tree,
but rooted in and out of time,
in court song and creation's prime,
in love that every moment makes the world.

4. *Strata Florida (2)*

for M

Hawthorn and rowan and outcrop rock
above us, and an autumn breeze
fluttering your hair,
your red hair, your grey hair.

What did I mean to say
taking you there, walking
among the tombs and hart's tongue fern,
looking into the love poet's yew,
the forest of branches?

Hawthorn and rowan burning
against rock on the hills around us
and your hair fluttering,
your grey hair, your red hair,
which the wind blew into flame.

5. *Imagining Wales*

for Emyr Humphreys

A peal of thunder, a fall of mist.
Afterwards the sun glares, staring on emptiness.
It ignites an image of fire
on ashen hearths, paints
evacuated rooms with streaks of red,
stains the ruined stronghold
on the promontory.

The machines are shrouded.
The quarries sink deeper
under the shadows of their walls.
The mineshaft is a dwelling for bats.

The man sits on the mound
and stares at his hands.
He turns them over, reads the lines on his palms.

He sleeps and his dream is a coracle
in which he is tossed on a stormy sea
that has drowned the cantrefs.
He peers out, into the spray
that stings his eyes,
and gradually, out of the waters,
a mountain takes shape.
He bows his head over his hands.

He is walking alone on the shore
but is not alone.
He kicks over wrack, examines the guillemot
that flaps like an oiled rag in the wash,
the beached seal with a hole in its side.
He wanders alone thinking of the broken walls,
the silence leaking in,
the men and women who sit staring
at the backs of their hands.

What can he do that they will remember?

He knows that memory is a place
that can be lost, though it lose nothing;
a place where all things remain
to be imagined anew.

He sits on the mound alone
and looks at the lines on his palms.

He sleeps and his dream is a coracle
in which he listens, listens hard
against the crash of waters
storming round and past – listens
where there are no words,
no symbol, no metaphor
to bear him over the torrent,
nothing but courage, and his mind
that listens, listens hard
against the fall of silence
crashing round and past . . .

A peal of thunder, a fall of mist.
Afterwards the sun appears
travelling on its daily round.
The man sits on the mound
and looks at the lines on his palms.

'That trees are men walking'

A poem dedicated to David Jones

Dry-mouthed,
in a dry time,
the polluted summer air grey,
I sit down to write a poem
I have been contemplating
for twenty years – an elegy.

And find nothing,
nothing to say
about death. For
the man who died is alive,
his images flow
in the channel that he made.

Yet there is a story to tell.

It begins with a bear,
a bear that the boy sees
in a London street,
a muzzled bear,
held on a chain,
a bear which he draws, dancing.

It is a story about a bear,
and about a boy who becomes a soldier.

A bear in a London street.
A soldier caught in a tangle
of barbed wire, torn khaki
exposing his private parts,
a human being in a place
that he shares with rats,
mules, shattered trees,
dead men,
trees that are men walking.

*

The artist mixes his saliva
with the pigment,
and spits on the cave wall.

It is not himself he paints,
but the living creatures.
But he is there, at one
with the herds that flow across the wall.

No doubt of it, no doubt at all –
he makes himself at home.
There he is, too, a figure
moving across the heavens –
the bear, and the hunter of the bear.

★

A ruffled air.
A closing among the trees,
the crucked branches fallen still.

Who was sitting there in his place?
(He was a child, but that was ages ago,
before the spit dried on the rockface.)

Whose scratch marks?
Whose pawprints?

Was it Artio, mother
of the Bear who rules the Honey Isle?

Trust him to recall the names,
more than the names,
this man of courage
who descends into the hades of oblivion,
who will leave none to perish.

Does Artio wake in the cave,
or is her body the cave
from which we issue,
emerging to read the scratch marks,

follow the pawprints,
going with care over the forest floor,
penetrating the tangle,
learning to dance?

*

Grandfather Bear

who gave his bones to the altar
his flesh to feed the tribe
his skin to clothe the being
who shifts his shape,
becomes the bear
who dances

Mother Bear

who digs under the roots,
makes herself a bed,
licks her paws, sleeps.
When she emerges, it is spring;
her cubs blink about her.
She licks them into shape.

Brother Bear

in a London street,
brown bear on a chain,
which the boy draws – dancing.

*

At Capel, in love
with the shape of things:

Dai, in his army greatcoat,
framed in a window, engraving.
Or walking with his friend
to unblock the stream
and free the waters.

Rhythm echoes rhythm
for the hunter of forms –
hill-shapes, trees,
hart's-tongue fern,
the horses that return
without riders –
the men betrayed to death.

Falling waters loose,
bind and loose,
shaping the ways of change.

And mist – mist crumbles rock.
Cloud packs hunt the hills.

Clouds, and mist, and something
that is neither,
a story of change woven
around the things that change.

That the dead men lie down
in the shattered wood,
shed their skins like snakes,
crawl back to the womb that bore them.

*

I paused by Nant Honddu,
by the dingle where David had a cell.

It was an enchanted place,
but what I saw was no dream.

The waters are dying, the trees
are being torn from the ground,
silt builds up in the rivers of the world,
the Thames, where he floated
the ark of his imagination,
the Rhine, the Danube
and the effluent of Europe,
the Brahmaputra,

the Nile, the Ganges,
the Euphrates, where Eden
is a desert of smoking wells.
We are making another earth;
the creatures we drew from the rock
are going back, fading,
their rhythm a distant beat.

Before the figures of the dance turn to stone,
before there is no voice left
to tell the story of the serpent
coiled around the mountains,
the serpent of drought
that Indra slew, freeing the waters,
before there is no hand to draw the bear,
no one to tell the wonder tale
of the bear waking in the cave,

pray for us, Dafydd.
David the Waterman,

pray for us.

Notes

'Westerbork'. The site of the former transit camp is now partly occupied by a radio astronomy centre, and the path through woods near the entrance is set out and measured as a model of the planets and their relative distances from one another.

'Vincent' draws some of its images from the letters of Vincent van Gogh.

'Edvard Munch: *The Sick Child*. Munch's words, which I use as an epigraph, are quoted from J. P. Hodin, *Edvard Munch* (Thames and Hudson, 1972).

'Verdun'. The words in italics quote, or adapt, translations of Franz Marc's words.

'Dreaming of Europe: a collage'. The quotation from Hans Arp is from his 'Dada Was Not a Farce' (Robert Motherwell, ed., *The Dada Painters and Poets*, The Belknap Press of Harvard University Press, 1981).

'Tel Gezer'. My second epigraph is from 'Gezer Diary', which consists of typescript accounts by Jewish survivors of the battle fought for Gezer on 10 June 1948, which destroyed the first kibbutz standing on the then border with Jordan, and of the events leading up to the battle, as the small group of survivors from Hitler's Europe coexisted uneasily (or failed to coexist) with Arab neighbours. When the battle eventually came, it was fought over ground that different peoples had died fighting over in wars or skirmishes throughout history, since times recorded in the Old Testament, and earlier. For Tel Gezer, rising above the kibbutz and partly on what is now its land, commands the valley of Aijalon, from which Jerusalem has always been vulnerable from attack, and has been held by – among others – Greeks and Jews and Romans, Crusaders and Muslims. I was lent a copy of the Diary while staying at the kibbutz, and as its words became part of my sense of the place, so some of them sound again in the poem, especially in part 5. For the most part, I have changed what I have taken from the Diary, but always with a view to revealing, as justly as possible in the circumstances in which no one has the right or the authority or the wisdom to stand in judgement over the events, the human truth of the people who in modern times converged and clashed in that place.

'Variations on a theme by Waldo Williams'. I would like to pay tribute to three sources. It was from Ned Thomas's book *The Welsh Extremist* that I first heard of Waldo Williams, in 1971. I do not now remember whether it was from the book or from Ned Thomas himself that I learnt about the poem in which Waldo Williams writes about the ancient skeleton of a young girl that he saw at Avebury. But it was in the book that I read the sentence, 'The fields are greener and the sea bluer because of the unseen company of past generations', which was influenced by Ned Thomas's reading of the Waldo Williams poem.

The second source is Tony Conran's translations of poems by Waldo Williams, especially 'Mewn Dau Gae'. This is a great poem in Welsh, but those who, like myself, do not have enough Welsh to read it in the original are indebted to Tony Conran for his translation, 'In Two Fields' (*Welsh Verse*, Poetry Wales Press, 1986), which is a great poem in English.

It was in James Nicholas's book on Waldo Williams in the Writers of Wales series (*Waldo Williams*, University of Wales Press, 1975) that I first read the lines that I use as an epigraph to my poem.

The fifth part of the 'Variations' borrows its image of 'a peal of thunder, a fall of mist' from *The Mabinogion.*

Reviewers on Jeremy Hooker

'Jeremy Hooker's achievement in these poems [*Solent Shore* 1978] is a great one, which I would set beside George Oppen's in his 'San Francisco Poems' or the late Lorine Niedecker's in her poems of Wisconsin. The effect is to suffuse the whole book with an emotion that is all the keener for never being explicitly formulated or invited: the emotion that we have when we recognize some particular terrain as "home" – that is to say, as an ample and enhancing arena in which lives can be lived that shall be truly "human", not merely "social". It is hard to think of a better, more humane or more timely, end for poetry to aim at.'

DONALD DAVIE, *PN Review*

'In many ways my favourite poet of all [in M. Schmidt, ed. *Some Contemporary Poets of Britain and Ireland*] is the quiet and delicate Jeremy Hooker, a poet American readers will like, I think, and one whose work has deep affinities with the Pound-Williams tradition.'

JOHN MATTHIAS, *Reading Old Friends*
(State University of New York Press, 1992)

'In the sure skill of his technique, and in the rare, intense consistency with which he treats themes which are obviously far more to him than the occasion for literature, he seems to be one of the best of our poets.'

DICK DAVIS, *Agenda*

Other books in the same series include

ANNA ADAMS *Green Resistance: New and Selected Poems*

SEBASTIAN BARKER *The Hand in the Well*

FRANCES CORNFORD *Selected Poems*

KEVIN CROSSLEY-HOLLAND *The Language of Yes*

KEVIN CROSSLEY-HOLLAND *Poems from East Anglia*

MARTYN CRUCEFIX *A Madder Ghost*

HILARY DAVIES *In a Valley of This Restless Mind*

DAVID GASCOYNE *Selected Prose*

DAVID GASCOYNE *Selected Verse Translations*

PHOEBE HESKETH *A Box of Silver Birch*

JUDITH KAZANTZIS *Swimming Through the Grand Hotel*

BLAKE MORRISON & PAULA REGO *Pendle Witches*

VICTOR PASMORE *The Man Within*

RUTH PITTER *Collected Poems*

JEREMY REED *Sweet Sister Lyric*

ANTHONY THWAITE *Selected Poems 1956-1996*

EDWARD UPWARD *Christopher Isherwood: Notes in Remembrance of a Friendship*

EDWARD UPWARD *The Scenic Railway*